Princess is Born

By

CHEURLIE PIERRE-RUSSELL

Publishing Information

Printed in the United States of America

Copyright © 2020

Cheurlie Pierre-Russell

Miami, Florida

All Rights Reserved

ISBN: 978-1-7350437-3-9

BOOKS BY C. PIERRE-RUSSELL

For Younger Readers:

Alani Story ABC Book

Little Kitty Goes to School

Sheila the Shy Shark

A Princess Is Born

Picture Books:

Broken Before the Storm

The Beauty of Love in Those We Shame

The Special Little Sister

Save the Missing Penny

Making Dollars Make Sense: Business Owner at Any Age

Friendly Monsters: Behind the Computer

For Older Readers:

The Better Betty

The Love of Likes

Butter Me Fly: My Way Home

Judge Me Now

Teens Soar in Their Credit Score

Today is a very special day. Jamiah and Jose learn that they will have a baby! This tiny baby is inside Jamiah's tummy, in a water-balloon-like sack where the baby will grow.

Jamiah gives her belly a hug and whispers, "My sweet Alani. We can't wait to meet you!" She knows that Princess Alani will not arrive for another six months, but Jamiah and Jose already love her dearly.

Now four months old,
baby Alani grows a
heart that starts
to beat!
Thump, thump.

She starts to wiggle
and wiggle around,
just a little.

Jose presses
his ear to
Jamiah's tummy
to listen for
their princess.

Jamiah's belly
starts to swell.
She loves the bump
her princess
is creating!

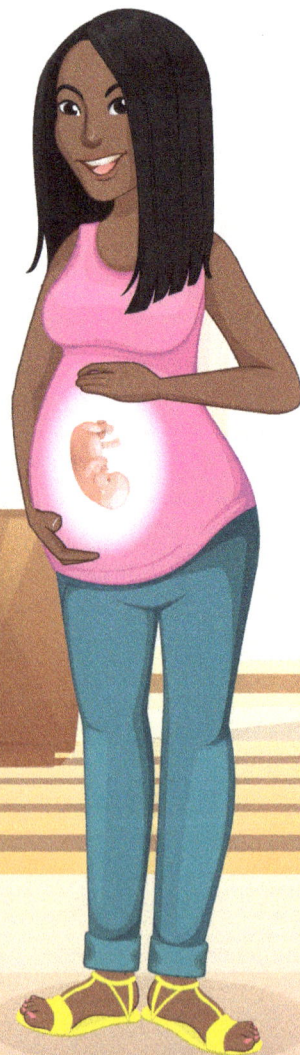

Princess Alani loves to squirm. She rolls around in her mother's belly more than before, flipping and twisting her body.

Alani grows fingers
and toes next.
She wiggles them
and even sucks
her thumb!
As her family
waits for her
arrival.

Time for an ultrasound! Jamiah and Jose go to see the doctor. The doctor uses a special tool to show the future parents their princess on a screen.
What will they see?

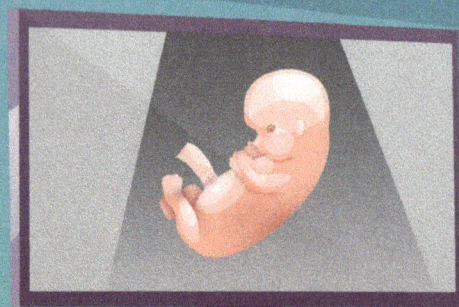

Look!
Princess Alani
also moves
her arms
from side
to side.
It looks like
she is
waving!

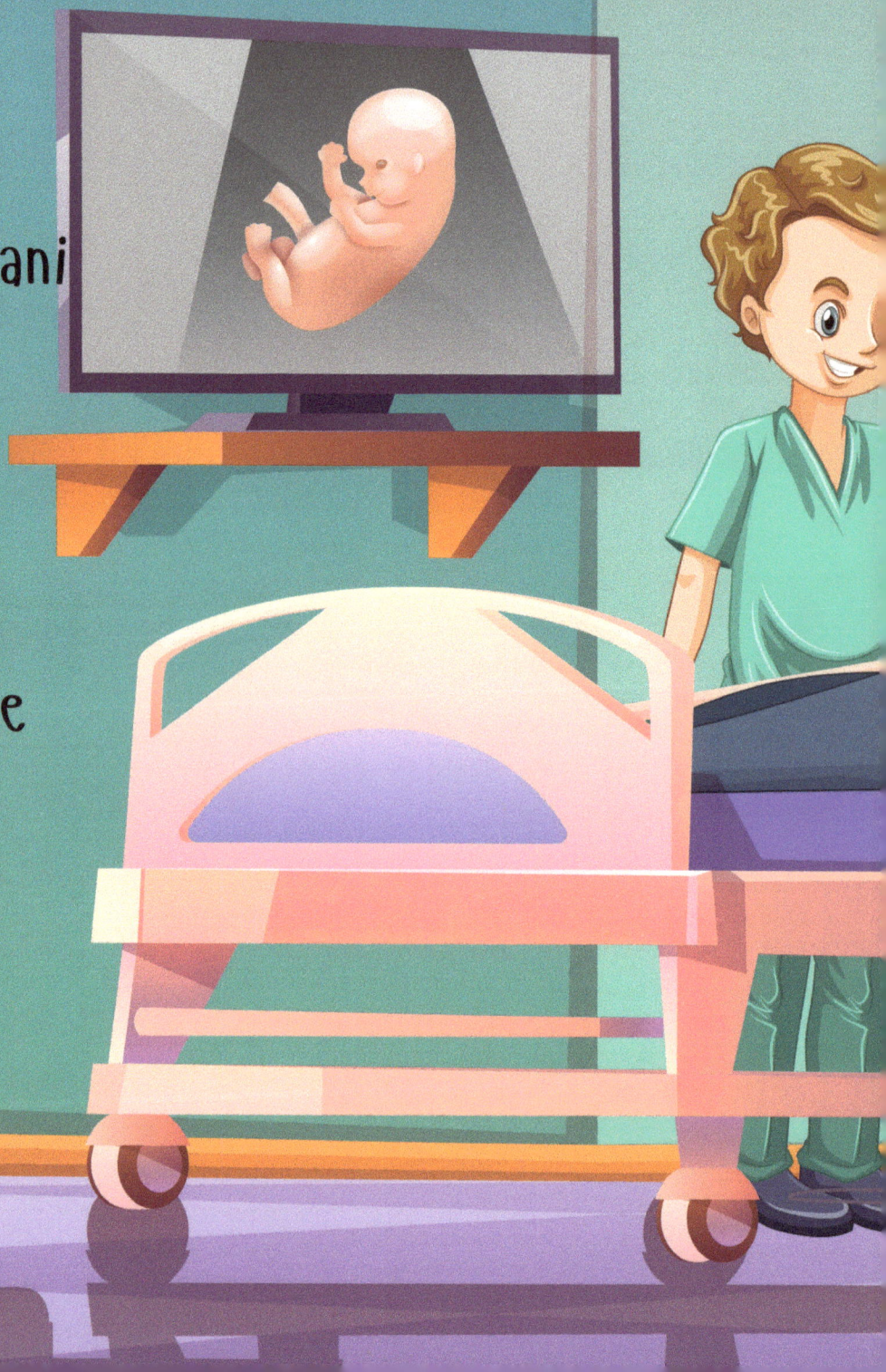

"Oh!"
Jamiah feels
her tummy jump.

Jose places a hand on her belly. Kick, kick, kick! Alani is having fun stretching her legs.

Perfectly safe
and snug inside
her mom, Alani
gives a smile.

Princess Alani hears her mom's voice. "I love you, princess," she says.

Hiccup! Princess Alani has the hiccups!
She makes her mom, Jamiah, jump with each hiccup!

It seems like Alani has her tap shoes on because she starts to kick like never before! She kicks and twists and flips and twirls. She keeps Jamiah awake at night with her "dancing."

Princess Alani has grown so much that Jamiah can't see her own toes. She can't reach them either. Jose helps Jamiah put her shoes on.

Together, they prepare the house. They know their princess will arrive any day now.

"Oof," Jamiah winces.
She is going into labor.
They rush to the hospital
with excitement.
Princes Alani is ready to
come into the world!

One, two, three and poof
she is here.
What a beautiful
princess she is.

Dedication

This one of a kind, hand-illustrated baby evolution book is written by Cheurlie Pierre-Russell, who dedicates this book to her granddaughter, Alani 'Story' Elize. This book is a gift you can open again and again. You are a gift your family will love more and more as time goes on. May your life be filled with beautiful stories and sweet dreams.

Alani Story Elize

About the Author

Cheurlie Pierre-Russell was born in Miami, Florida, in 1976 and is the author of several books for children and adolescents. Cheurlie publishes highly visual, photographic fiction and nonfiction for children and teens. A veteran of the United States Navy, she graduated from Miami Edison Senior High School.

After receiving her bachelor's degree in sociology from Georgia State University, she later obtained a master's degree in psychology from Walden University. Her combined areas of interest in sociology and psychology influenced her mission: to inform, educate, and entertain children to help them overcome life challenges through her writing. Cheurlie brings unrivaled clarity to a wide range of topics with a unique combination of words and pictures, put together to spectacular effect. A strong role model for women and children, Cheurlie is a wife and has three amazing children of her own.

www.ingramcontent.com/pod-product-compliance
Lightning Source LLC
Chambersburg PA
CBHW041601260326
41914CB00011B/1340